THIS

Content PLANNER

BELONGS TO

Social Media Planner

Sunday				
Monday				
Tuesday				
Wednesday				
Thursday				
Friday				
Saturday				

Content Planner

Title

Call to Action

Description

To Do List

Publish Date

Social Platform

Type / Category

Key Words

Links to Include

Content Planner

Title

Call to Action

Description

To Do List

Publish Date

Social Platform

Type / Category

Key Words

Links to Include

Content Planner

Title
_____

Call to Action
_____

Description

_____
_____
_____
_____
_____
_____
_____
_____
_____
_____
_____
_____
_____
_____

To Do List

_____
_____
_____
_____
_____

Publish Date

Social Platform

Type / Category

Key Words

Links to Include

Content Planner

Title
_____

Call to Action
_____

Description
_____
_____
_____
_____
_____
_____
_____
_____
_____
_____
_____
_____

To Do List
_____
_____
_____
_____
_____
_____

Publish Date

Social Platform

Type / Category

Key Words

Links to Include

Content Planner

Title _____

Call to Action _____

Description

_____
_____
_____
_____
_____
_____
_____
_____
_____
_____
_____
_____

To Do List

_____
_____
_____
_____
_____
_____

Publish Date

Social Platform

Type / Category

Key Words

Links to Include

Content Planner

Title
_____

Call to Action
_____

Description

_____
_____
_____
_____
_____
_____
_____
_____
_____
_____
_____
_____
_____

To Do List

_____
_____
_____
_____
_____

Publish Date

Social Platform

Type / Category

Key Words

Links to Include

Content Planner

Title
_____

Call to Action
_____

Description
_____
_____
_____
_____
_____
_____
_____
_____
_____
_____
_____

To Do List
_____
_____
_____
_____
_____
_____

Publish Date

Social Platform

Type / Category

Key Words

Links to Include

Social Post Planner

Date

Image ☐ Time

Caption

Keywords

Notes

Date

Image ☐ Time

Caption

Keywords

Notes

Social Post Planner

Date

ⓕ ⓘ ⓣ ⓟ ▷   Image ☐   Time

Caption

Keywords

Notes

Date

ⓕ ⓘ ⓣ ⓟ ▷   Image ☐   Time

Caption

Keywords

Notes

Social Post Planner

Date

Image ☐   Time

Caption

Keywords

Notes

Date

Image ☐   Time

Caption

Keywords

Notes

Social Post Planner

Date

Time

Image ☐

Caption

Keywords

Notes

Social Media Planner

Sunday				
Monday				
Tuesday				
Wednesday				
Thursday				
Friday				
Saturday				

Content Planner

Title
_____

Call to Action
_____

Description

_____
_____
_____
_____
_____
_____
_____
_____
_____
_____
_____
_____

To Do List

_____
_____
_____
_____
_____
_____

Publish Date

Social Platform

Type / Category

Key Words

Links to Include

Content Planner

Title
_____

Call to Action
_____

Description
_____
_____
_____
_____
_____
_____
_____
_____
_____
_____
_____
_____
_____

To Do List
_____
_____
_____
_____
_____
_____

Publish Date

Social Platform

Type / Category

Key Words

Links to Include

Content *Planner*

Title
_____

Call to Action
_____

Description
_____
_____
_____
_____
_____
_____
_____
_____
_____
_____
_____

To Do List
_____
_____
_____
_____
_____

Publish Date

Social Platform

Type / Category

Key Words

Links to Include

Content Planner

Title
_____

Call to Action
_____

Description

_____
_____
_____
_____
_____
_____
_____
_____
_____
_____
_____
_____
_____
_____

To Do List

_____
_____
_____
_____
_____

Publish Date

Social Platform

Type / Category

Key Words

Links to Include

Content Planner

Title

Call to Action

Description

To Do List

Social Platform

Type / Category

Key Words

Links to Include

Content Planner

Title
_____

Call to Action
_____

Description
_____
_____
_____
_____
_____
_____
_____
_____
_____
_____
_____
_____

To Do List
_____
_____
_____
_____
_____

Publish Date

Social Platform

Type / Category

Key Words

Links to Include

Content Planner

Title

_____

Call to Action

_____

Description

_____
_____
_____
_____
_____
_____
_____
_____
_____
_____
_____

To Do List

_____
_____
_____
_____
_____

Publish Date

Social Platform

Type / Category

Key Words

Links to Include

Social Post Planner

Date

Image ☐   Time

Caption

Keywords

Notes

Date

Image ☐   Time

Caption

Keywords

Notes

Social Post Planner

Image ☐ Time

Caption

Keywords

Notes

Date

Image ☐ Time

Caption

Keywords

Notes

Social Post Planner

Date

Image ☐ Time

Caption

Keywords

Notes

Date

Image ☐ Time

Caption

Keywords

Notes

Social Post Planner

Date

Image ☐ Time

Caption

Keywords

Notes

Social Media Planner

Sunday				
Monday				
Tuesday				
Wednesday				
Thursday				
Friday				
Saturday				

Content Planner

Title

Call to Action

Description

To Do List

Publish Date

Social Platform

Type / Category

Key Words

Links to Include

Content *Planner*

Title
_____

Call to Action
_____

Description

_____
_____
_____
_____
_____
_____
_____
_____
_____
_____
_____
_____
_____
_____

To Do List

_____
_____
_____
_____
_____
_____

Publish Date

Social Platform

Type / Category

Key Words

Links to Include

Content *Planner*

Title

_____

Call to Action

_____

Description

_____
_____
_____
_____
_____
_____
_____
_____
_____
_____
_____
_____
_____

To Do List

_____
_____
_____
_____
_____
_____

Publish Date

Social Platform

Type / Category

Key Words

Links to Include

Content Planner

Title
_____

Call to Action
_____

Description

_____
_____
_____
_____
_____
_____
_____
_____
_____
_____
_____
_____
_____

To Do List

_____
_____
_____
_____
_____
_____

Publish Date

Social Platform

Type / Category

Key Words

Links to Include

Content _Planner_

Title
_____

Call to Action
_____

Description
_____
_____
_____
_____
_____
_____
_____
_____
_____
_____
_____
_____

Social Platform

Type / Category

Key Words

To Do List
_____
_____
_____
_____
_____

Links to Include

Content Planner

Title
_____

Call to Action
_____

Description
_____
_____
_____
_____
_____
_____
_____
_____
_____
_____
_____
_____
_____
_____
_____

To Do List
_____
_____
_____
_____
_____
_____

Publish Date

Social Platform

Type / Category

Key Words

Links to Include

Content Planner

Title

_____

Call to Action

_____

Description

_____
_____
_____
_____
_____
_____
_____
_____
_____
_____
_____
_____
_____

To Do List

_____
_____
_____
_____
_____

Publish Date

Social Platform

Type / Category

Key Words

Links to Include

Social Post Planner

Date

Image ☐

Time

Caption

Keywords

Notes

Date

Image ☐

Time

Caption

Keywords

Notes

Social Post Planner

Date

Image ☐ Time

Caption

Keywords

Notes

Date

Image ☐ Time

Caption

Keywords

Notes

Social Post Planner

Date

Facebook Instagram Twitter Pinterest YouTube Image ☐ Time

Caption

Keywords

Notes

Date

Facebook Instagram Twitter Pinterest YouTube Image ☐ Time

Caption

Keywords

Notes

Social Post Planner

Date

Image ☐   Time

Caption

Keywords

Notes

Social Media Planner

Sunday				
Monday				
Tuesday				
Wednesday				
Thursday				
Friday				
Saturday				

Content Planner

Title

Call to Action

Description

To Do List

Publish Date

Social Platform

Type / Category

Key Words

Links to Include

Content *Planner*

Title

_____

Call to Action

_____

Description

_____
_____
_____
_____
_____
_____
_____
_____
_____
_____
_____
_____

To Do List

_____
_____
_____
_____
_____
_____

Publish Date

Social Platform

Type / Category

Key Words

Links to Include

Content Planner

Title
_____

Call to Action
_____

Description

_____
_____
_____
_____
_____
_____
_____
_____
_____
_____
_____
_____

To Do List

_____
_____
_____
_____
_____

Publish Date

Social Platform

Type / Category

Key Words

Links to Include

Content Planner

Title
_____

Call to Action
_____

Description
_____
_____
_____
_____
_____
_____
_____
_____
_____
_____
_____
_____
_____

To Do List
_____
_____
_____
_____
_____

Publish Date

Social Platform

Type / Category

Key Words

Links to Include

Content Planner

Title

Call to Action

Description

To Do List

Social Platform

Type / Category

Key Words

Links to Include

Content *Planner*

Publish Date

Title
_____

Call to Action
_____

Social Platform

(f) (Instagram) (Twitter) (Pinterest)
(LinkedIn) (Play) (Mail)

Description

_____
_____
_____
_____
_____
_____
_____
_____
_____
_____
_____
_____

Type / Category

Key Words

Links to Include

To Do List

_____
_____
_____
_____
_____

Content Planner

Title
_____

Call to Action
_____

Description
_____
_____
_____
_____
_____
_____
_____
_____
_____
_____
_____
_____
_____

To Do List
_____
_____
_____
_____
_____

Publish Date

Social Platform

Type / Category

Key Words

Links to Include

Social Post Planner

Date

Image ☐ Time

Caption

Keywords

Notes

Date

Image ☐ Time

Caption

Keywords

Notes

Social Post Planner

Date

Image ☐   Time

Caption

Keywords

Notes

Date

Image ☐   Time

Caption

Keywords

Notes

Social Post Planner

Date

Image ☐ Time

Caption

Keywords

Notes

Date

Image ☐ Time

Caption

Keywords

Notes

Social Post Planner

Date

Image ☐

Time

Caption

Keywords

Notes

Social Media Planner

Sunday				
Monday				
Tuesday				
Wednesday				
Thursday				
Friday				
Saturday				

Content Planner

Title

_____

Call to Action

_____

Description

_____
_____
_____
_____
_____
_____
_____
_____
_____
_____
_____
_____

To Do List

_____
_____
_____
_____
_____

Publish Date

Social Platform

Type / Category

Key Words

Links to Include

Content Planner

Title
_____

Call to Action
_____

Description
_____
_____
_____
_____
_____
_____
_____
_____
_____
_____
_____
_____

To Do List
_____
_____
_____
_____
_____
_____

Publish Date

Social Platform

Type / Category

Key Words

Links to Include

Content Planner

Title

Call to Action

Description

To Do List

Social Platform

Type / Category

Key Words

Links to Include

Content Planner

Title
_____

Call to Action
_____

Description
_____
_____
_____
_____
_____
_____
_____
_____
_____
_____

To Do List
_____
_____
_____
_____

Publish Date

Social Platform

Type / Category

Key Words

Links to Include

Content Planner

Title
_____

Call to Action
_____

Description

_____
_____
_____
_____
_____
_____
_____
_____
_____
_____
_____
_____
_____

To Do List

_____
_____
_____
_____
_____

Publish Date

Social Platform

Type / Category

Key Words

Links to Include

Content Planner

Title
_____

Call to Action
_____

Description

_____
_____
_____
_____
_____
_____
_____
_____
_____
_____
_____
_____
_____
_____

To Do List

_____
_____
_____
_____
_____

Publish Date

Social Platform

Type / Category

Key Words

Links to Include

Content Planner

Title

Call to Action

Description

To Do List

Publish Date

Social Platform

Type / Category

Key Words

Links to Include

Social Post Planner

Date

◯f ◯ ◯ ◯ ◯▷ Image ☐ Time

Caption

Keywords

Notes

Date

◯f ◯ ◯ ◯ ◯▷ Image ☐ Time

Caption

Keywords

Notes

Social Post Planner

Date

Image ☐

Time

Caption

Keywords

_____ _____

_____ _____

_____ _____

_____ _____

_____ _____

Notes

_____

Date

Image ☐

Time

Caption

Keywords

_____ _____

_____ _____

_____ _____

_____ _____

_____ _____

Notes

_____

Social Post Planner

Date

Image ☐ Time

Caption

Keywords

Notes

Date

Image ☐ Time

Caption

Keywords

Notes

Social Post Planner

Date

Image ☐

Time

Caption

Keywords

Notes

Made in the USA
Las Vegas, NV
21 April 2022

47808044R00070